99 Bible Promises for Tough Times

99 Bible Promises for Tough Times

Randy Petersen

WaterBrook
PRESS

99 BIBLE PROMISES FOR TOUGH TIMES
PUBLISHED BY WATERBROOK PRESS
12265 Oracle Boulevard, Suite 200
Colorado Springs, Colorado 80921

All Scripture quotations, unless otherwise indicated, are taken from the *Holy Bible, New International Version*®. NIV®. Copyright © 1973, 1978, 1984 by International Bible Society. Used by permission of Zondervan Publishing House. All rights reserved. Scripture quotations marked (KJV) are taken from the King James Version.

Details in some anecdotes and stories have been changed to protect the identities of the persons involved.

ISBN 978-0-307-45838-4
ISBN 978-0-307-45844-5 (electronic)

Copyright © 2009 by WaterBrook Multnomah Publishing Group

All rights reserved. No part of this book may be reproduced or transmitted in any form or by any means, electronic or mechanical, including photocopying and recording, or by any information storage and retrieval system, without permission in writing from the publisher.

Published in the United States by WaterBrook Multnomah, an imprint of the Crown Publishing Group, a division of Random House Inc., New York.

WATERBROOK and its deer colophon are registered trademarks of Random House Inc.

Library of Congress Cataloging-in-Publication Data
Petersen, Randy.
   99 Bible promises for tough times / Randy Petersen.—1st ed.
      p. cm.
   ISBN 978-0-307-45838-4 — ISBN 978-0-307-45844-5 (electronic) 1. Suffering—Biblical teaching. 2. Bible—Quotations. 3. God (Christianity)—Promises. I. Title.
   BS680.S854P48 2009
   242'.5—dc22
                                                        2009011975

Printed in the United States of America
2009—First Edition

10 9 8 7 6 5 4 3 2 1

SPECIAL SALES
Most WaterBrook Multnomah books are available at special quantity discounts when purchased in bulk by corporations, organizations, and special-interest groups. Custom imprinting or excerpting can also be done to fit special needs. For information, please e-mail SpecialMarkets@WaterBrookMultnomah.com or call 1-800-603-7051.

Contents

Introduction 1

1. When You Face Financial Difficulties 3

2. In Times of Poor Health 17

3. When You Have Anxiety or Conflict 33

4. When You Struggle with Sin and Guilt 47

5. When God Seems Far Away 59

6. Challenges in Your Work and Service 71

7. When You Lose a Loved One 85

Introduction

> For everything that was written in the past
> was written to teach us, so that through
> endurance and the encouragement
> of the Scriptures we might have hope.
> —ROMANS 15:4

Maybe you know someone who always has a positive outlook. No matter what misfortunes occur, this person is always looking on the bright side. When you go through a time of suffering, this person is always ready with a cheery word.

Maybe you secretly want to strangle that person.

This is not a book of happy denial for difficult situations. It's not about turning pessimism to optimism or finding the silver lining in every mist. Life is tough. And if you've been watching the news lately, you know it may be getting tougher. If we're going to get through these problems, we have to get *through* them. We can't tap-dance around them. Maybe Little Orphan Annie can get away with that as she convinces President Roosevelt that "the sun'll come up tomorrow," but this ain't Broadway. We're knee-deep in real life.

One great thing about the Bible is that it confronts real life. It stands up to real issues. The Old Testament character Job faces every catastrophe you can think of, but as he pleads his case with God, he still sings, "I know that my Redeemer lives" (19:25). The apostle Paul lists all the beatings, arrests, and shipwrecks he has endured, he tells about his unanswered prayer, and he still hears God saying, "My power is made perfect in weakness" (2 Corinthians 12:9).

God's promises come out of gritty situations, so they can speak to your gritty situations. He doesn't always tell you what you want to hear, but he always seems to change the camera angle. If you're locked on today's problems, he'll show you tomorrow. If you're worried about tomorrow, he'll show you eternity.

Your tough times may be personal or relational, financial or health-related. Maybe you have suffered a loss or you fear you soon will. Whatever your difficulty is, God promises to meet you there.

1 When You Face Financial Difficulties

"The economy is hitting us hard," said one woman to her best friend. "No vacation this year. We were going to go to Disney World, but now we'll just be renting a few cartoons on DVD. Not quite the same thing."

"I know what you mean," her friend replied. "Our house is now worth less than our mortgage. I think our 401(k) is now a 201(k)."

It's nice when you can laugh about it, but spiraling economic woes are wreaking havoc in many families. Layoffs, cutbacks, reductions in pay—it's tough all over.

And we're not just talking about some numbers in a bankbook. Economic issues affect basic questions of our lives. Can you send your kids to college? Will you have to work another decade before retiring? Can you squeeze a few more years out of your current clunker before getting a new car? It's only natural to worry about these things.

Except Jesus told us not to.

Money was one of Jesus's most frequent subjects. He challenged people to focus on God rather than their pocketbook. How can we worry about money when the Creator of all good things has promised to care for us?

Stock markets go up and down. People get hired and fired. Nest eggs sometimes get stolen by swindlers. That's why Jesus told us to deposit our treasure—and our hearts—in heaven. No matter how iffy the economy, God is a sure thing. We can always count on his promises.

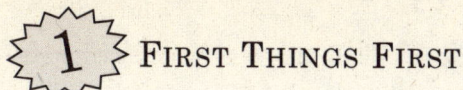 First Things First

> But seek first his kingdom and his
> righteousness, and all these things
> will be given to you as well.
> —Matthew 6:33

Jesus had just been chiding his listeners for worrying too much. "What shall we eat?" "What shall we wear?" And if you're fretting that you won't be able to afford the latest fashions this spring, Jesus has advice for you: look at the lilies of the field. "Not even Solomon in all his splendor was dressed like one of these" (Luke 12:27). And if God provides such amazing styles for simple plants, what will he provide for you?

The key, Jesus said, is to put first things first. Don't spend your energy obsessing over your wardrobe or your menu, but focus on how God wants you to live. Let him be your king. And then he'll take care of all these other necessities of life.

 Delight and Desire

> Delight yourself in the LORD
> and he will give you the desires of your heart.
> —Psalm 37:4

On their honeymoon, the groom looked over as his bride enjoyed a spectacular sunset. "I love to see you being happy," he said.

Thinking that over for a moment, she replied, "That's going to work out pretty well then, isn't it?"

She was right. If his main desire was to bring her delight, then whenever she was happy, he would be happy too. Of course it was still just the honeymoon.

The psalmist is saying the same sort of thing about our relationship with God. At face value, you might take this promise as a kind of blank check. "Lord, I want a house, a car, a vacation." But when we find delight in the Lord, we want what he wants. We just want to make him happy.

3 Payback

> And my God will meet all your needs according
> to his glorious riches in Christ Jesus.
> —Philippians 4:19

The apostle Paul knew all about economic hardship. "I know what it is to be in need," he told the Philippians (verse 12), but there were also times of plenty. He had learned to be content whether rich or poor.

In these personal comments at the end of this letter to the church at Philippi, Paul thanked them for some gifts they had sent.

Like many of us, he probably wished he could get them a return gift, but he was in prison at the moment. It wasn't easy to run out to Wal-Mart for a little something.

Instead, he asked God to return the favor on his behalf. He knew the Lord had more than enough "glorious riches" to meet their needs, just as Paul's own needs were being met—thanks to their generosity.

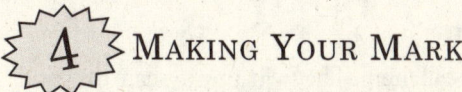# MAKING YOUR MARK

> The world and its desires pass away, but the man
> who does the will of God lives forever.
> —1 JOHN 2:17

"Everything I've worked for. Gone." The man was watching the stock market slide with alarm. He was heavily invested, and his shares were tumbling in value. "That's the fortune I was going to leave my kids."

Our recent economic troubles have caused similar heartache with many parents who were trying to build a legacy, something their children could live on in the future. But what is the best legacy? What fortune really lasts? Not money or the things it can buy. The apostle John reminds us that our lasting treasure comes from doing what God wants. That's an inheritance that will enrich your children's lives forever. Maybe we can all use this time to refocus on what really matters.

5 24/7

> Keep your lives free from the love of money and be
> content with what you have, because God has said,
> "Never will I leave you;
> > never will I forsake you."
> > —HEBREWS 13:5

"Fair-weather friends," we call them. They're happy to share the good times with us, but when things go sour, they're otherwise engaged. The anguish of the current crisis is just made worse by the sense of neglect, even betrayal, from these so-called friends. But God isn't like that. He's with us 24/7, always ready to respond to our prayers.

This promise from the book of Hebrews doesn't seem to connect right away. What does God's faithfulness have to do with loving money? Think about it. Can money make the same promise? No, the almighty dollar *often* forsakes us. We're far better off with a heart full of God than a handful of money.

6 20/20

> Listen, my dear brothers: Has not God chosen those who
> are poor in the eyes of the world to be rich in faith and to
> inherit the kingdom he promised those who love him?
> > —JAMES 2:5

James had just given a hypothetical example: Suppose a rich man walks into your church. You'd give him the best seat in the house, making a poor man sit on the floor. This is wrong, James says. It's nearsighted.

Sure, the world sees the rich man as the most important person in the room, but God sees differently. Jesus often said that, in God's kingdom, the first would be last and the last first. He called the poor "blessed," perhaps because they get to trust God for everything.

If you're worried because financial problems are threatening to make you poor, put on the specs of James 2:5 and see things from God's perspective.

 ## This Is a Test

"Bring the whole tithe into the storehouse, that there may be food in my house. Test me in this," says the LORD Almighty, "and see if I will not throw open the floodgates of heaven and pour out so much blessing that you will not have room enough for it."
—MALACHI 3:10

The Israelites were commanded to bring the first tenth of their harvest to the temple. This tithe was offered to God as a way of saying that he was more important than anyone else. But in Malachi's time, people were neglecting this obligation. So God dared them with this extravagant promise.

When our finances get tight, it's easy to cut down on our donations to church and charities. But what if we were to take that dare, to continue making God the first priority in our shrinking budget? What blessings could we expect?

 ## Reading the Will

> Blessed are the meek,
> for they will inherit the earth.
> —Matthew 5:5

It's a familiar movie scene: the greedy family gathering for the reading of the rich man's will. They're shocked when the entire estate goes to…the humble housekeeper.

That's the picture Jesus offers. In a world that prizes toughness, ambition, reaching for what you want, and knocking everyone else out of the way, the earth will be inherited by…the meek. These are the people who don't force their will upon others. They put others first. They don't grab; they give.

You might feel humbled by your financial circumstances. Maybe you're blaming yourself for being *too* meek, for not being more cutthroat in your business dealings. But Jesus maps out a different pathway to success. In due time, God's entire estate will be willed to…you.

9. Disaster Plan

> Cast your bread upon the waters,
>   for after many days you will find it again.
> Give portions to seven, yes to eight,
>   for you do not know what disaster may come
>   upon the land.
> —ECCLESIASTES 11:1–2

Ecclesiastes is the most depressing book of the Bible, so it's no surprise to find a reference to disaster. Yet there's a promise in these verses, as well as a strategy. You might think that casting your bread on the waters will yield only moldy bread, but the author probably meant exporting grain to overseas trading partners.

A sense of impending disaster might tempt you to hoard what you have, but this promise invites you to share it, invest it, spread it around. Give freely to those around you, and in your time of need you'll see your resources coming back to you.

10. Satisfied

> Let them give thanks to the LORD for his unfailing
>   love
>   and his wonderful deeds for men,

> for he satisfies the thirsty
> and fills the hungry with good things.
> —PSALM 107:8–9

Kids crave candy. You might have experienced the incessant whining that goes on at the checkout counter of a supermarket or convenience store. Smart parents know that an overdose of candy spells trouble, but children don't. They're convinced that the parent who says no is the meanest ogre on earth.

The same dynamic often occurs between us and God, except we're on the younger end of that exchange. "Lord, why won't you give me this? I want it! If you loved me, you'd give it to me!" But the Lord promises to fill us with "good things"—not whatever we want, but the things that truly satisfy.

 GOOD WORK

> God is able to make all grace abound to you, so that
> in all things at all times, having all that you need,
> you will abound in every good work.
> —2 CORINTHIANS 9:8

Ray worked for a struggling company, so he didn't say much when he sat day after day at an obsolete computer. It had a painfully slow Internet connection and couldn't run many cutting-edge programs because it just didn't have the memory. Finally he told his boss, "I know money's tight, but I could work so much better if I had better equipment. I don't need luxury. I just want to do good work."

That's the idea we find in 2 Corinthians. We're called to help others, give to the needy, and share the good news, and God gives us what we need to do the "good work" he wants us to do.

 Laptop

Give, and it will be given to you. A good measure, pressed down, shaken together and running over, will be poured into your lap.

For with the measure you use, it will be measured to you.

—LUKE 6:38

We have shopping carts nowadays. Food comes prepackaged in specified amounts. This promise gives us a snapshot of everyday life a few millenniums ago. Back then, we'd buy grain at the market, where it was measured out by the seller and poured into the folds of our garments.

Jesus says that a spirit of giving comes back to help us. If we are generous to others, then the people we deal with will be generous to us, not only giving us what we pay for, but also pressing it down to make room for more, and topping it off for "good measure."

Don't let a tight budget tighten your heart too. Show grace and you'll receive it.

13. Prisoners of Hope

Return to your fortress, O prisoners of hope;
even now I announce that I will restore twice as
much to you.
—Zechariah 9:12

The bottom dropped out for the residents of Judah as the mighty Babylonians swept through their land, taking their money, their leaders, and finally *them*. They had considered their capital, Jerusalem, an impregnable fortress, but now it lay in ruins, their temple smoldering. For seventy years they languished in Babylon, with dreams of returning home. New generations were brought up with that hope in their hearts.

"Prisoners of hope," the prophet called them, and there's a deep double meaning. Of course these captives held the hope of returning, but in a way, the hope held them. That's true today too. When you trust the Lord, no matter how bad things get, the hope still holds you. The Lord will restore.

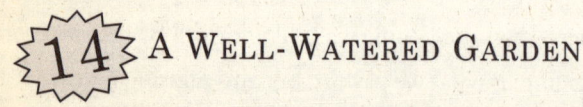

14. A Well-Watered Garden

The Lord will guide you always;
he will satisfy your needs in a sun-scorched land

> and will strengthen your frame.
> You will be like a well-watered garden,
> like a spring whose waters never fail.
> —ISAIAH 58:11

Jim was a brash college student on a study tour in Israel when he decided to hike from Jerusalem to Jericho. The arid climate was even more so with the summer heat as Jim followed the dry waterways through the canyons of the Judean desert. He had several canteens with him, but he was still rationing his water carefully.

At one point he rounded a bend and came upon a lush green garden, a well-irrigated oasis. Water fell into the streambed there—melted snow from the mountains—and children were splashing in a pool.

This is the Lord's promise. Your dry life will grow green again.

2 In Times of Poor Health

It's no fun to be sick. There's often pain, or at least discomfort, and boredom if you're bedridden. Sometimes it's embarrassing. You can't do some things you want to do. You have to trundle off to doctors' offices and remember to take medicine. You don't feel like yourself. You might worry about others catching your disease. You might worry about what you're missing while you recuperate. You might worry that you'll never recuperate.

Poor health also puts us in an interesting position with God. He's a healer, we know, so we pray for healing. We trust, we demand, we bargain, we question. *Don't you want me to be the best I can be? Then why this?* We worry that we don't have enough faith to be healed. Of course there are always well-meaning but tactless friends with a range of dubious advice.

The promises of God always seem to be bigger than what we're looking for. We want to get fixed up, back in the saddle, good as new. But God expresses concern for our inner lives as well as our physical health. Does he let our bodies languish so he can fix up our souls? Maybe sometimes. He keeps talking about eternity, too, as if he's in no great hurry to make us better. He reminds us often that we're headed to a place of perfect health. His promises may not always provide the answers we want, but they consistently take us somewhere, deeper into his mind and heart.

 Renewal

> Therefore we do not lose heart. Though
> outwardly we are wasting away, yet inwardly
> we are being renewed day by day.
> —2 Corinthians 4:16

Maybe you have a favorite old mug. Into it you pour your morning coffee, your afternoon tea, or your bedtime cocoa. It might be stained, dulled by many washings, chipped, or cracked—but it still warms your hand as you enjoy its contents day by day.

That mug is like you. Outwardly we show the chips and cracks of everyday wear and tear, but inwardly we are renewed daily with the outpouring of the Spirit. Just before this promise of renewal, the apostle Paul described us as "jars of clay" (see verse 7), perhaps thinking about Adam being fashioned from the dust of the earth. We are indeed earthen vessels, but don't focus on the fading exterior. Feel the warmth of what God is pouring into you.

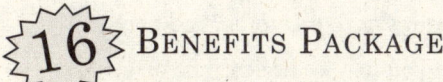 Benefits Package

> Praise the LORD, O my soul;
>   all my inmost being, praise his holy name.

> Praise the LORD, O my soul,
> and forget not all his benefits—
> who forgives all your sins
> and heals all your diseases,...
> who satisfies your desires with good things
> so that your youth is renewed like the eagle's.
> —PSALM 103:1–3, 5

You might be thinking about benefits a lot these days if your health plan is (or isn't) paying for your doctor visits and hospital stays. Companies hire us with promises of extensive health coverage; only later do insurance companies show us the fine print.

The psalmist advertises God's benefits package, which includes not only the healing of disease but also the forgiveness of sin. Scripture often puts our inner and outer needs together, and that makes sense. As you recuperate physically, make sure you explore the healing power of forgiveness too.

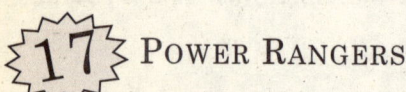

POWER RANGERS

> Therefore confess your sins to each other and pray
> for each other so that you may be healed. The prayer
> of a righteous man is powerful and effective.
> —JAMES 5:16

Prayer has power. James mentions Elijah, whose prayers called down fire from heaven. Because he was some spiritual giant? No. James says he was "just like us" (verse 17).

Scholars suggest that Christians took over the Roman Empire through prayer, not prayers for political overthrow, but for healing. Even when it was illegal for Christians to gather openly, they became known as healers. A Roman family might send for a Christian nurse to provide care for a sick child—and prayer. This even happened in some emperors' families.

Someone like you has changed the world through prayer. Why not take this opportunity to pray with Christian friends for both spiritual and physical needs? Then stand back and see what happens.

18. Senior Moments

> Even to your old age and gray hairs
> > I am he, I am he who will sustain you.
> > I have made you and I will carry you;
> > I will sustain you and I will rescue you.
>
> —Isaiah 46:4

Fifty is the new forty, they say. Sixty-year-olds look like they're fifty, or at least they try to. Denial reigns in our culture. Hair dye, wrinkle cream, and hip replacements are selling like there's no tomorrow.

But there is a tomorrow. Despite our desperate attempts to look, feel, and act younger, each of us is growing older, day by day.

That's why the Lord's promise is so precious. He doesn't care about our graying heads or our wrinkling skin. He still loves us, and he will sustain us. It's a rough road we tread, getting older, but God says he will carry us.

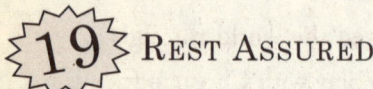 REST ASSURED

> I will lie down and sleep in peace,
> for you alone, O LORD,
> make me dwell in safety.
>
> —PSALM 4:8

Ginny had a problem with migraine headaches. They were often triggered by job stress and made worse by lack of sleep. Medication seldom worked. The best thing was to get a good night's rest, but that was difficult when her head was pounding. A headache would last two or three days, limiting her productivity and creating even more pressure at work.

Maybe you have experienced similar cycles. Sleep is an important part of the healing process for many ailments, but sometimes it's hard to come by. Writing this psalm, David was facing not only the pressure of executive decision making but also the constant threat of enemy ambush. Yet he could rest in the confidence that God was in control. And so can we.

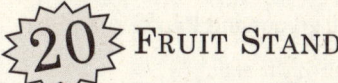 Fruit Stand

> The righteous will flourish like a palm tree,
>> they will grow like a cedar of Lebanon;
> planted in the house of the LORD,
>> they will flourish in the courts of our God.
> They will still bear fruit in old age,
>> they will stay fresh and green,
> proclaiming, "The LORD is upright;
>> he is my Rock, and there is no wickedness in him."
>
> —Psalm 92:12–15

At seventy-nine, Irma struggles with painful arthritis that limits her movements. She has long served as a Sunday school teacher and Bible study leader, but now she can't get out to church much. *How can God use me now?* she wonders.

This promise assures her that she can "still bear fruit," though maybe in new, creative ways. Perhaps through phone calls, conversation with visitors, prayer, and her gift of sharing stories of God's goodness she can still proclaim that the Lord is her rock.

21 ⟩ HERE COMES THE SUN

> But for you who revere my name, the sun
> of righteousness will rise with healing
> in its wings. And you will go out and leap
> like calves released from the stall.
>
> —MALACHI 4:2

Imagine being cooped up all winter. Maybe you've been ill and confined to bed. Maybe the weather's been so frightful you just couldn't venture out. But one day the sun is shining and the calendar says it's spring. You decide to take a walk. Once outside, you just bask in the brightness. The sun's warmth fills your pores. As your spirit soars, your walking turns to skipping, then to dancing.

This is how Malachi describes God's plans for his people. Many see this as a prophecy about Christ or about God's coming kingdom, but it might also depict the everyday joy of a loving relationship with the Lord.

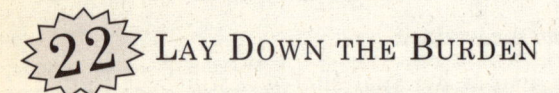

22 ⟩ LAY DOWN THE BURDEN

> Come to me, all you who are weary
> and burdened, and I will give you rest.
>
> —MATTHEW 11:28

Scientists have established a link between stress and poor health. When you are under great pressure, your immune system suffers, not to mention the effect of stress on blood pressure. Highly stressed people tend to make bad decisions with regard to eating, smoking, drinking alcohol, or other risky behaviors. Often the things they do to relieve stress only create more.

Unfortunately, modern life is full of stress—at work, at home, in the community. Is there any sane way to cope?

Jesus invites us to come to him for relief. What does that mean? Praying. Meditating on his words. Following his example in loving others. Trusting him for strength in tough times. In these ways and more, when stress threatens our health, we can rest in him.

23. When No One Cares

> "But I will restore you to health
> and heal your wounds,"
> declares the LORD,
> "because you are called an outcast,
> Zion for whom no one cares."
> —JEREMIAH 30:17

Sickness can have its advantages. Sometimes people fuss over you, showing kindness they'd never show when you're healthy. Sometimes, when a temporary illness puts you out of action, people realize that they take you for granted. Co-workers understand how important you are to the company. Your family sees all that you do in the home.

But our suffering can intensify when *no one* seems to care. You sense life going on without you, and nobody even knows you're missing. Here the Lord assures his people that he cares, even if no one else does. In fact, it seems he offers special care to the outcast *because* of the neglect of others. You can find powerful comfort in that.

24. ME, MYSELF, AND I

> And after my skin has been destroyed,
>> yet in my flesh I will see God;
> I myself will see him
>> with my own eyes—I, and not another.
>> How my heart yearns within me!
>> —JOB 19:26–27

Job had lost everything, and he sat in the ashes, scratching his diseased skin while three friends tried to figure out what he had done wrong. Maybe you feel like Job these days, wondering why you're suffering. Maybe your friends help you analyze the situation—like it or not.

In this promise, however, Job grabs a personal pronoun and won't let go. I myself. Me. He clung to his personal relationship with God. His friends could float their hypothetical arguments, but he knew that someday he would see God face to face, in stark reality. Whatever your friends say, it comes down to just you—and God.

25. HOMEWARD BOUND

> But our citizenship is in heaven. And we eagerly
> await a Savior from there, the Lord Jesus Christ,
> who, by the power that enables him to bring
> everything under his control, will transform our lowly
> bodies so that they will be like his glorious body.
> —PHILIPPIANS 3:20–21

Maybe you know the old spiritual that goes, "This world is not my home, I'm just a-passin' through." In this promise, the apostle Paul reminds us of that fact. Heaven is home to us now. We are being transformed by the power of Christ.

In times of illness, it's easy to focus on "our lowly bodies." They're just not performing up to our standards! But take a moment to get a glimpse of the heavenly plane. There we'll have new bodies, free of sickness and death. That will truly be home, sweet home.

 ## My Way

> Heal me, O LORD, and I will be healed;
> save me and I will be saved,
> for you are the one I praise.
>
> —JEREMIAH 17:14

Jeremiah was a reluctant prophet with an unpopular message. He knew people would react badly to God's message, but he still proclaimed it and suffered for it. Much of the book of Jeremiah consists of a running dialogue with God about the prophet's various misfortunes—imprisonment, slander, plots against his life. He didn't deserve any of it—and he regularly reminds God of that fact. *Here's what you should do, Lord.*

Maybe you carry on a dialogue like that. Heal me, O Lord! And then everyone will see I've been healed. By you. And it will prove that you're God and I'm with you. Wouldn't that be great?

It's fine to have that conversation. Just recognize that God might have a better idea.

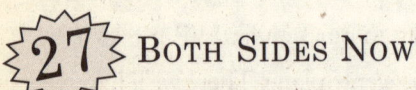 ## Both Sides Now

> My heart is glad and my tongue rejoices;
> my body also will rest secure,

> because you will not abandon me to the grave,
> nor will you let your Holy One see decay.
> You have made known to me the path of life;
> you will fill me with joy in your presence,
> with eternal pleasures at your right hand.
> —PSALM 16:9–11

Peter used this passage as a prophecy of Jesus's resurrection, but it's also a stirring proclamation of faith for any believer. Does it mean we won't die? Of course not. But God won't abandon us, even at death. He has set us on a "path of life," and we will walk it right into his presence.

Eternal life isn't just hereafter; it has already started! Our bodies can "rest secure," even in bad health, because we know our life with God will continue.

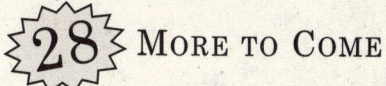 MORE TO COME

> I am with you and will watch
> over you wherever you go, and I will
> bring you back to this land.
> I will not leave you until I have done
> what I have promised you.
> —GENESIS 28:15

Jacob was homeless at the moment, on the run and scared to death. He had just cheated his brother out of the family fortune, and Esau vowed revenge. So Jacob skipped town, looking over his shoulder. Did I mention that Esau was good at hunting?

When he finally stopped for the night, Jacob had a strange dream of a stairway to heaven. God spoke to him with this promise. *There's more to come,* he seems to be saying. *I'm not finished with you yet.*

Whether you're eighteen or eighty, the same message comes to you. God fulfills his promises—to you and through you—every day of your life.

29 PORTIONS

> My flesh and my heart may fail,
> but God is the strength of my heart
> and my portion forever.
>
> —PSALM 73:26

The psalmist uses a great term for God—"my portion"—and it requires some explanation. We know the word. We buy products in particular portions (which seem to be decreasing in size), and we take our income and pay the government a portion (which seems to be increasing in size). Is that all God is—a part of our life experience?

Not at all. Imagine that someone brings you a pizza and says,

"Take all you want." You select one big piece, loaded with all the toppings you love. "That's all I need," you say. It's a portion of the pizza, but it completely satisfies you. That's what this word means to the psalmist. Even in times of physical and emotional distress, God is completely enough.

30. CONTAGIOUS

> Surely goodness and love will follow me
> all the days of my life,
> and I will dwell in the house of the LORD
> forever.
>
> —PSALM 23:6

Esther was hospitalized in the last days of her earthly life, losing a long battle with cancer. Her daughter came from far away to be with her, and she was amazed at what she found. Doctors and nurses were dropping by Esther's room just to talk. Even in the face of death, this woman had a contagious joy about her. She was asking about issues in her visitors' lives and offering to pray for them. What was going on here? Goodness and love had followed Esther all her life, and they weren't quitting now. Even to the last day, she radiated these godly qualities.

In your time of physical need, you can let those same qualities touch others.

3 When You Have Anxiety or Conflict

Life is hard and love is harder.

That's a rather dour perspective, but when things start going wrong, it's just what we feel. Daily existence gives us plenty of things to worry about, and relationships just intensify the issue. Whether we're concerned about our kids, fighting with a spouse, or recovering from a friend's betrayal, we struggle to find peace.

But peace is exactly what the Lord promises, not only interpersonal accord but also an inner sense of calm. God is there for us even when no one else is. God loves us even when we feel unlovable. God has great plans for us even when we're sure our future has slammed shut.

Let the Lord's promises into your heart. Trust him to heal your wounds. Allow him to transform not only your mind and morals but also your feelings.

31 A Different Peace

> Peace I leave with you; my peace I give you.
> I do not give to you as the world gives. Do not let
> your hearts be troubled and do not be afraid.
> —JOHN 14:27

The evening before the crucifixion, Jesus was preparing the disciples for his departure. He had already promised that the Holy Spirit would live within them. And then he promised them peace, taking pains to define this peace as something special, something different from the world's brand.

Remember that the Hebrew word for hello and good-bye is *shalom,* which means "peace." It's not just a word, Jesus might have been saying, but my powerful gift to you. Or was he scoffing at the *Pax Romana,* the "peace" the Romans had won with their brutality?

The world may offer you various solutions to your emotional turmoil. The Prince of Peace offers a change of heart.

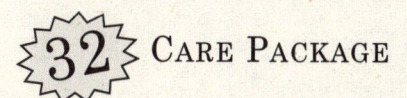

32 Care Package

> Cast all your anxiety on him because
> he cares for you.
> —1 PETER 5:7

Peter was once in a fishing boat when a terrible storm blew up. Jesus was sleeping through it—until the disciples roused him with their cry, "Don't you care if we drown?" (Mark 4:38). What a question for the Lord of love! Of course he cared.

But that's how we react to a crisis too, isn't it? The storm blows up and we worry that God is asleep somewhere, unconcerned. So we take it upon ourselves to fix things, instead of trusting the Lord to lead us.

When the disciples in that boat finally let Jesus take charge, they saw him rebuke the storm as if he were scolding a toddler: "Quiet! Be still!" (verse 39). And everything went calm. The same sort of thing happens today as people toss their anxiety toward Jesus.

33 Bones

> The LORD is close to the brokenhearted
> > and saves those who are crushed in spirit.
> A righteous man may have many troubles,
> > but the LORD delivers him from them all;
> he protects all his bones,
> > not one of them will be broken.
>
> —PSALM 34:18–20

Some Scripture verses make it seem that a believer's life will be problem-free, but in its totality the Bible acknowledges the struggles we all face. Our faith will not prevent our hearts from breaking, but the Lord promises to stay close to us when that happens. Troubles will occur even in a righteous life, but the Lord works within those situations to help us.

Some football teams have found success with a bend-but-don't-break defense. That is, they give up yards but not points. That might be the Lord's strategy too. Spiritually speaking, our bones may bend, but he doesn't let them break.

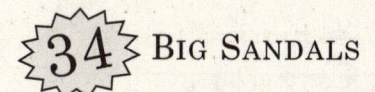

34 Big Sandals

> Have I not commanded you? Be strong
> and courageous. Do not be terrified;
> do not be discouraged, for the LORD your God
> will be with you wherever you go.
> —Joshua 1:9

Moses had led the Israelites for forty years. A whole generation had grown up with Moses as their only leader. Stories were told of Moses confronting the Pharaoh and demanding freedom. Moses outconjured the magicians of Egypt. He parted the sea. He met the Lord at the burning bush. He knew God on a first-name basis.

But Moses had died and now it was time for his successor, Joshua. Gulp. He had big sandals to fill.

Maybe you know what that's like, facing a big task without

much of a track record. According to this promise, we can move forward with confidence, not in our own ability, but in the God who goes with us.

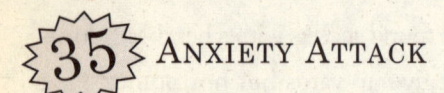

35. Anxiety Attack

> Do not be anxious about anything, but in
> everything, by prayer and petition, with
> thanksgiving, present your requests to God.
> And the peace of God, which transcends
> all understanding, will guard your hearts
> and your minds in Christ Jesus.
> —Philippians 4:6–7

"Don't worry, be happy." The song still tumbles easily through our consciousness as the island beat lulls us into a pleasant optimism. Is that what the apostle Paul is setting forth here, just a positive mental outlook, a shrugging assurance that everything will turn out all right? Not exactly.

Prayer replaces anxiety. We have plenty to be worried about, but we package it up and ship it off to God. Then *his* peace guards over our hearts. Ironically, the term *guard* is a military one. God's peace stands as a sentry, barring the way to any secret agent of anxiety that might creep into our hearts.

36. NEW AS DEW

> Because of the LORD's great love we are not
>   consumed,
> for his compassions never fail.
> They are new every morning;
> great is your faithfulness.
> I say to myself, "The LORD is my portion;
> therefore I will wait for him."
> The LORD is good to those whose hope is in him,
> to the one who seeks him;
> it is good to wait quietly
> for the salvation of the LORD.
> —LAMENTATIONS 3:22–26

The city lay in ruins. Jerusalem had fallen to the Babylonian military machine, and the smoke was still rising. The author of Lamentations vividly depicts the damage done, expressing sorrow over the nation's sin.

Then, stunningly, in the middle of this lament, a new day dawns. The author takes a moment to celebrate the Lord's faithfulness, the compassions that are "new every morning."

Whatever pain you have endured, start the new day by looking for God's goodness.

37 No Fear

> The LORD is my light and my salvation—
> whom shall I fear?
> The LORD is the stronghold of my life—
> of whom shall I be afraid?
>
> —PSALM 27:1

Sandra ventured into the city to audition for a play, not sure where to go or what to do. But at the theater she saw Carolyn, an old college chum. After some small talk, Carolyn began instructing Sandra—fill out a form, give it to that person, go through that door, listen for your name. Sandra was already feeling more confident, but then she asked, "Why don't you have a form? Aren't you auditioning?"

"No," said Carolyn. "I'm the director."

Then Sandra knew she had nothing more to fear, since she knew the person in charge. In this psalm, David is saying, if the Lord is guiding you, what is there to fear?

38 Peace

> You will keep in perfect peace
> him whose mind is steadfast,
> because he trusts in you.
>
> —ISAIAH 26:3

What do you do when you don't know what to do? Circumstances often come up that baffle us. We waver between options, sometimes unable to do anything. A New Testament verse talks about the "double-minded man, unstable in all he does" (James 1:8).

The verse from Isaiah looks at this from the opposite side. What happens when your mind is steadfast, when you commit yourself totally to trusting the Lord? You still may not know everything, but you act on the knowledge you have. Wherever God guides you, you will go.

The result, Isaiah says, is "perfect peace." In Hebrew, the word *peace* is just doubled, a way of expressing intensity. The Lord keeps us in *shalom shalom* when we unwaveringly commit ourselves to him.

39. Inseparable

> For I am convinced that neither death nor life, neither
> angels nor demons, neither the present nor the future,
> nor any powers, neither height nor depth, nor
> anything else in all creation, will be able to separate us
> from the love of God that is in Christ Jesus our Lord.
>
> —ROMANS 8:38–39

When our human relationships go bad, we long even more deeply for the love of God. Our friendships, romances, even marriages have their ups and downs, and sometimes they break apart, but

Scripture assures us that God's love is a sure thing. Nothing in this world or the next can break us up.

The apostle Paul wrote this stunning promise in a chapter where he discussed suffering, in a book where he discussed sin. The conclusion is clear: your suffering does not mean God has stopped loving you, and your sin will not deter his love.

40 Forgive Us Our Trespasses

> For if you forgive men when they sin against you,
> your heavenly Father will also forgive you.
> —Matthew 6:14

Jesus tacked this addendum onto the Lord's Prayer, and it's a little puzzling. It sounds as if we have to do this righteous deed—forgiving others—in order to deserve God's forgiveness. But the New Testament clearly says that we can never deserve God's forgiveness. It's a free gift of God's grace.

Yet there's a deep wisdom in this promise. When we open our hearts to forgive others, we're more open to receive God's grace. Perhaps you know people who are constantly keeping score, holding grudges against all who have wronged them. Isn't it hard for them to humbly seek God's forgiveness when they're standing in judgment of these others?

Open your heart to your trespassers, and then enjoy the free gift of forgiveness.

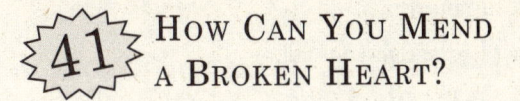

41. How Can You Mend a Broken Heart?

> He heals the brokenhearted
> and binds up their wounds.
> —Psalm 147:3

"I will never, ever, love anyone ever again!"

The teenage girl's boyfriend just ditched her for a classmate, right before their three-month anniversary. In her adolescent way, she had been sure that he would cherish her forever. She had practiced writing her name with his last name. She had shared with him her innermost thoughts and dreams. But now he was gone, and she was deeply wounded.

Adults smile knowingly at such puppy love, because we've known that pain ourselves. Loving is risky business. Hopes can quickly get dashed.

The psalmist reminds us that God is in the business of healing our hearts. Whether it's a three-month thing or a thirty-year marriage, the Lord assures us that we are loved, that we have value, that we have a purpose. He strengthens us to love again.

42. I'll Take Care of All That

> Cast your cares on the LORD
> and he will sustain you;
> he will never let the righteous fall.
> —PSALM 55:22

Nearly eighty years old, Amanda saw her health failing and worried that she couldn't manage life alone in her home anymore. But where would she move and when? Her mind began racing with a million concerns.

"I'll take care of all that," said her son Kurt. "You can move in with me if you want."

"Yes, but how would we pack up everything? Who would move it all? And can we sell the house in this market?"

"I'll take care of all that," Kurt repeated. The next day he created a detailed schedule that assuaged her worries.

We see the same thing in this promise, as God asks us to let him bear our cares.

43. Comfort

> Praise be to the God and Father of our Lord Jesus
> Christ, the Father of compassion and the God of all

> comfort, who comforts us in all our troubles, so that
> we can comfort those in any trouble with the
> comfort we ourselves have received from God. For
> just as the sufferings of Christ flow over into our
> lives, so also through Christ our comfort overflows.
> —2 CORINTHIANS 1:3–5

"Why, God, why?" we ask when things go wrong—broken relationships, tragic accidents, unexpected losses. We seek some reason to make sense of it.

This promise provides several helpful clues. It describes Jesus's sufferings flowing into us, suggesting that we understand our Lord better when we have to suffer too. We also receive God's comfort, which draws us even closer to him. And often we find some purpose when we comfort others who are suffering as we have suffered.

4 When You Struggle with Sin and Guilt

Guilt is a gift.

That might be hard to accept, but it's true. God has wired us with a sense of guilt as a kind of moral thermostat. When we have done something wrong, those guilt feelings kick in. We know we have to deal with them.

Problems occur when our guilt sensors are too touchy or too numb. Some feel guilty over every little thing, and they carry remorse for sins confessed long ago. Others get so used to certain sins that they no longer recognize that they're wrong.

Sin and guilt will mess up your life—both unfounded feelings of guilt and actual habitual sins. But this is God's specialty. The many promises of Scripture indicate that he is eager to forgive our sins, to assuage our guilt, and to transform our behavior. If these are your struggles, let him speak to you.

44 WE NEED TO TALK

> "Come now, let us reason together,"
> says the LORD.
> "Though your sins are like scarlet,
> they shall be as white as snow;
> though they are red as crimson,
> they shall be like wool."
>
> —ISAIAH 1:18

When you're in a serious relationship, four little words can strike terror in your heart: "We need to talk." This usually means one partner is upset with something the other partner has no clue about.

God says the same thing here, but it is a positive thing. Up until this point, the first chapter of Isaiah is pretty rough. "Stop bringing meaningless offerings!" the Lord pleads. "Your incense is detestable to me" (verse 13). All efforts to appear religious were annoying him.

The conversation had simply lacked an honest admission of guilt. Once they owned up to their sin, he would be happy to cleanse them. Once we own up to our sins, he is happy to cleanse us.

45 DUST

> He will not always accuse,
> nor will he harbor his anger forever;

> he does not treat us as our sins deserve
>> or repay us according to our iniquities.
> For as high as the heavens are above the earth,
>> so great is his love for those who fear him;
> as far as the east is from the west,
>> so far has he removed our transgressions from us.
> As a father has compassion on his children,
>> so the LORD has compassion on those who fear him;
> for he knows how we are formed,
>> he remembers that we are dust.
>> —PSALM 103:9–14

Perhaps the most stirring part of this amazing psalm is the reference to dust. God formed the first human from the dust of the earth, so when we fall short of heavenly perfection, he understands. Sure, he wants us to do right, but when we don't, he's ready to forgive.

46. EVERYTHING OLD IS NEW AGAIN

> Therefore, if anyone is in Christ, he is a new creation; the old has gone, the new has come!
> —2 CORINTHIANS 5:17

Makeovers have been all the rage on television lately. Whether it's your face, figure, or fashion sense, there's some so-called expert who promises a "new you." Of course these external changes can't change your heart, but that's precisely what God promises to do.

In Christ, we're told, anyone can become a whole new creation. Old habits, old attitudes, old allegiances get made over into a sparkling new life.

If you're weighed down with feelings of guilt, this promise is for you. Bring those burdens to the cross of Christ and let the Lord transform you. Let bygones be bygones and welcome the brand-new possibilities of life lived in Christ's power and love.

47. Justice Served

> If we confess our sins, he is faithful and just
> and will forgive us our sins and purify
> us from all unrighteousness.
> —1 John 1:9

A student comes late to class and the teacher's supposed to send her to the office, but the student says, "I'm really sorry. Could you bend the rules for me this once?" Let's say the teacher ignores the lateness. That teacher is being faithful to the student perhaps, but not being *just*.

The promise of 1 John 1:9 tells us that God doesn't bend the rules to forgive us, but he operates according to his divine justice. Jesus has paid the penalty for our sins on the cross. No more penalty is due. So when we confess that we've done wrong and deserve punishment, God just stamps PAID on our account and forgives us. Because of Jesus's sacrifice, God's justice is served.

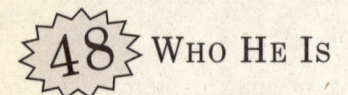

48. Who He Is

> If we are faithless,
> he will remain faithful,
> for he cannot disown himself.
> —2 Timothy 2:13

From the playgrounds of our childhood we learned the basic principle of retribution: be mean, and people will be mean to you. But God's grace challenges that notion. We wrong him, but he still showers us with love.

The early Christians faced a tough dilemma. While many of them endured brutal persecution for their faith, others buckled under, giving in to their torturers' demands, denying their faith or sacrificing to the Roman gods. After the danger had passed, what was to be done with those who had proven faithless in tough times?

This promise, from an early church creed, explains that God does not retaliate in kind. When our faithfulness fails, his remains strong. He is, eternally, who he is. And he is a God of grace.

49. Confidence

> Let us then approach the throne of grace with
> confidence, so that we may receive mercy
> and find grace to help us in our time of need.
> —Hebrews 4:16

Say you're a midlevel business executive meeting with your boss for a performance review. You might be incredibly nervous, or you might walk into that office with confidence. It all depends on your relationship with that boss.

The book of Hebrews takes Jewish traditions and applies them to Jesus. In this picture, Jesus is that boss, a high priest who loves and understands us. He knows the challenges we have dealt with. And he takes us *with him* into the holy of holies, the special place known as the mercy seat, where the Israelites received atonement for their sins.

Normally this would scare us silly, but Jesus is right there beside us. His understanding gives us the confidence we need.

50. Deliver Us from Evil

> But the Lord is faithful, and he will strengthen
> and protect you from the evil one.
> —2 Thessalonians 3:3

Nowadays the idea of the Evil One, the devil, seems strange to people, a throwback to old mythology. Yet Scripture warns us of an agent of evil that prowls the earth like a lion, seeking to devour us. Such warnings put the fear of the devil in some believers, who look for demonic influence in every computer glitch or allergic sniffle. But we also receive regular assurance in Scripture that our God is greater than any evil force out there.

"Lead us not into temptation," we often pray, "but deliver us from evil." The promise from 2 Thessalonians confirms that he will do just that. So, while evil forces—tempters and enemies—will seek to drag you down, you can trust the Lord for protection.

51. Clean Sweep

> I will sprinkle clean water on you, and you
> will be clean; I will cleanse you from all
> your impurities and from all your idols.
> —Ezekiel 36:25

When you swim in the ocean, you might come out feeling refreshed, but you don't feel clean. Why? Because the ocean is full of salt, sand, and who knows what else. You probably want to take a shower afterward, and in fact many beaches have showers nearby to sprinkle clean water on you.

In this promise of restoration, the Lord offers cleansing from impurities. His people had strayed into idol worship with its various nefarious practices, and now he wanted them back. The thing about idols is that they pretend to offer cleansing, but they don't really cleanse. That's true of modern idols too—money, success, pleasure. After bathing in those pursuits, you still need the clean shower of God's love.

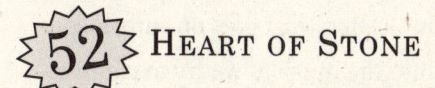

52 Heart of Stone

> I will give you a new heart and put a new
> spirit in you; I will remove from you your
> heart of stone and give you a heart of flesh.
> And I will put my Spirit in you.
> —Ezekiel 36:26–27

Growing up in a Christian home, Claudia learned the truth about God. She continued going to church into young adulthood, believing all the doctrines—but she always had issues. Claudia loved God, but she had a keen eye for hypocrisy, and she resisted becoming a "cookie-cutter Christian."

One day she prayed, "Lord, I serve you with my mind and body, but my heart is hard. Please melt it, at least a little." In the next church service, Claudia felt the old urge to critique everything, but she stopped. Instead, she tried to open up to God's wooing. The melting had begun.

53 Mud Pit

> Return, faithless people;
>   I will cure you of backsliding.
> —Jeremiah 3:22

Backsliding. It sounds like a game on *Survivor*. Put people in a mud pit and let them try to climb out. Is that what goes on with us spiritually? Are we slipping back into the muck as we try to climb toward God? The Hebrew word that Jeremiah used is a lot more intentional. It's a "turning," as if we got safely out of the mud pit and climbed right back in. God rescues us from sin, but we keep turning back. He parts the sea to deliver us from slavery, but then we want to go back to Egypt—not unlike the celebrity who gets out of rehab and starts using again.

Yet here God promises a cure, and the New Testament confirms it. His Spirit can truly transform our desires.

54 Snowballs

> My son, do not despise the LORD's discipline
>   and do not resent his rebuke,
> because the LORD disciplines those he loves,
>   as a father the son he delights in.
> —Proverbs 3:11–12

Three little boys are throwing snowballs at passing cars. A car stops. A man steps out. "Don't you know how dangerous that is?" He sends two boys home, but he grabs Johnny by the wrist. "I'm taking you home right now." He is Johnny's father, already planning an appropriate punishment.

Why do two boys escape scot-free while Johnny has to suffer? Does Dad love Johnny less? No, more.

Sometimes God disciplines us, making life difficult, or at least allowing us to reap the negative results of our sins. Is this because he has stopped loving us? On the contrary. He is showing his love through discipline, helping us grow into the disciples he wants us to be.

55 Parachute

> To him who is able to keep you from falling and
> to present you before his glorious presence
> without fault and with great joy—to the only
> God our Savior be glory, majesty, power and
> authority, through Jesus Christ our Lord,
> before all ages, now and forevermore! Amen.
> —Jude 1:24–25

Some people jump out of airplanes. For fun. Joy celebrated her sixty-fifth birthday by going skydiving, something she had always wanted to do, to the horror of her friends and family. "You don't know anything about skydiving," they said.

"I don't have to," Joy responded. "There's a guide who jumps with me. He stays connected with me. He will keep me from falling."

Living can be pretty dangerous, at least if we're doing it right, but the Lord is committed to our eternal safety.

56 Escape Hatch

> God is faithful; he will not let you be tempted
> beyond what you can bear. But when you
> are tempted, he will also provide a way out
> so that you can stand up under it.
> —1 Corinthians 10:13

Adam set the pattern for all of us. When God confronted him about the original sin, he immediately passed the buck, accusing "the woman you put here with me" (Genesis 3:12). It's easy for us to blame God for putting irresistible temptations in our path, but that argument won't fly. Whatever temptations we encounter, there's always a way out.

That functions both as a promise and as a challenge. You have the strength to stand up to temptation or to run away from it. So when you're tempted, instead of assuming your inevitable failure, start looking for the escape hatch.

5 When God Seems Far Away

You may have seen a poster or bumper sticker that says, "If God seems far away from you, guess who moved." It's certainly clever, but not quite right. The saying assumes that this distant feeling is always caused by our own sin or neglect. But the experience of many believers throughout the ages, and even in the Bible, says otherwise.

Yes, sometimes we drift away from God, but other times he truly seems to withdraw from us. It's as if he's a young lover playing hard to get. Not that he stops loving us—never that—he just wants us to seek him. When his presence is always obvious to us, we can begin to slack off in our attention. The challenge of seeking him, of listening for a softer voice, of looking for more obscure signs, is good for us. Ultimately we deepen in our love for him, but the process can be difficult.

If you're in the midst of that process, you're probably feeling all sorts of unpleasant doubts and fears. You need to cling to these promises.

57 HIDE-AND-SEEK

> "You will seek me and find me when
> you seek me with all your heart. I will be
> found by you," declares the LORD.
> —JEREMIAH 29:13–14

Surely you played hide-and-seek as a child. There is joy in finding a good hiding place, but sometimes it's *too* good. You don't want your friends to have to search for hours. They'll give up the game! Eventually you do want to be found.

This game is a fitting picture of our relationship with God. Sometimes we hide from him—as Adam and Eve did in the Garden of Eden—and sometimes he hides from us. Hiding creates a challenge. It forces us to consider: is this person worth looking for?

When we say yes, and when we truly seek him, he will be found. That's his promise.

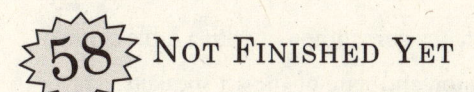

58 NOT FINISHED YET

> Being confident of this, that he who began
> a good work in you will carry it on to
> completion until the day of Christ Jesus.
> —PHILIPPIANS 1:6

At a groundbreaking ceremony, the first shovel is shoved into the earth and we envision the future edifice. We endure traffic delays for road construction, knowing that the finished product will speed us on our way. We open the garage door and sigh over the massive cleanup required, but then we start on it. Progress may be impeded by weather conditions, labor strikes, or personal distractions, but the job has begun, and it will get done.

You might feel that God started your spiritual growth and then went on vacation. Then hear this promise. He will finish the job. You can be utterly confident of that.

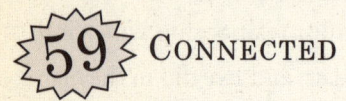

59 Connected

> I am the vine; you are the branches.
> If a man remains in me and I in him, he will bear
> much fruit; apart from me you can do nothing.
> —John 15:5

As a retiree, Bob bought a fancy new computer with a cable connection, a big flat-screen monitor, and state-of-the-art speakers. Maybe he overspent, but it was time he entered the twenty-first century.

Home from the store, he eagerly assembled his new purchase and pushed the On button. Nothing happened. Angrily he called the store and was put on hold. Then he called his son, who came over and discovered the flaw. It wasn't plugged in.

You may be a very impressive person with gifts and capabilities galore, but if you're not getting much done, check your connection. If you're not plugged into Jesus, that may be the problem. If you are, the possibilities are amazing.

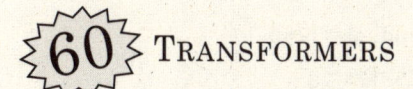

60 Transformers

> Do not conform any longer to the pattern
> of this world, but be transformed by the
> renewing of your mind. Then you will be
> able to test and approve what God's will is—
> his good, pleasing and perfect will.
> —ROMANS 12:2

Many Christians get paralyzed on this question: what does God want? It's frustrating when we seek God's will for important decisions, but we don't receive any special revelation. Without any voice from heaven or angelic visits, how do we know what we should do?

This promise has two layers to it: transformation and information. It starts with the questions of who we are and who we are becoming. Will we squeeze into the world's predictable ways, or will we let God transform us into someone entirely new and surprising?

Once transformed, with a renewed mind, we have a new ability to grasp the desires of God.

61. Reality Show

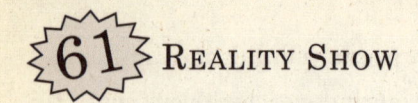

> Blessed is the man whom God corrects;
> so do not despise the discipline of the Almighty.
> For he wounds, but he also binds up;
> he injures, but his hands also heal.
> —Job 5:17–18

Parenting gives great insight into God's relationship with us. Some experts have talked lately about reality discipline, saying that kids should experience the results of their actions. If you tell your son to wear a sweater on a cold day and he refuses, you might want to let him shiver for a while. But there's a limit. Eventually you might give him your own sweater. That's not reality discipline. It's just love.

God parents us in both ways, allowing us to face some negative consequences of our sin, but also stepping in with loving support. From our childish perspective, we might think his reality discipline is unfair, but it's just as valuable as the healing.

62. Distress Call

> But if from there you seek the LORD your God,
> you will find him if you look for him with all your
> heart and with all your soul. When you are in

> distress and all these things have happened to you,
> then in later days you will return to the LORD your
> God and obey him. For the LORD your God is a
> merciful God; he will not abandon or destroy you.
> —DEUTERONOMY 4:29–31

The Bible has few stories of people who always got everything right. Instead, it gives numerous examples of rebellion and return. People have ups and downs with God. Sometimes the Lord seems far away, and sometimes people drift away from him. We are urged to stay close to God, but there's always a plan B. Deuteronomy files this promise away for a future time of distress, and you can too.

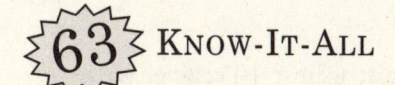

63 KNOW-IT-ALL

> This then is how we know that we belong to the
> truth, and how we set our hearts at rest in his
> presence whenever our hearts condemn us. For God
> is greater than our hearts, and he knows everything.
> —1 JOHN 3:19–20

We go through cycles of faith and doubt. There are times when we question everything we thought we knew about God. Then we feel guilty for doubting, and that just continues the cycle of self-condemnation.

But the apostle John says that faith isn't just in your mind; it's in your actions. When you say a kind word to a neighbor, when you work in an inner-city soup kitchen, when you tend the church nursery, you are expressing your faith in Christ. You may think you don't really know anything about God anymore, but rest assured that he knows you and loves you.

64. Clueless

> The Spirit helps us in our weakness. We do not know
> what we ought to pray for, but the Spirit himself
> intercedes for us with groans that words cannot express.
> —Romans 8:26

Sometimes our prayers seem to splat against the ceiling. We have no clue what to pray for. We can ask for success in this project or that venture, but is that really what God wants? Won't his will be done whether or not we say those words?

But here we are promised that our prayers are just one end of an elaborate spiritual process. The Spirit translates our weak requests into an inexpressible language of passion and petition.

So if you feel that you're just not speaking God's language, you're right. But maybe language isn't necessary. Send some heartfelt groans in the Spirit's direction and see what happens.

65. Rebirth Certificate

> The Spirit himself testifies with our spirit
> that we are God's children.
> —Romans 8:16

When God seems far away, it can shake you. The basic assumptions of life are absent. The ground on which you walk feels fragile, like thin ice. Take God out of the equation, and there is nothing solid.

You begin to wonder who you are. If God is irrelevant, does that mean you are just a concoction of chemicals, a beast on an evolutionary ladder, driven by animal impulses? Just where have you come from and where are you going? Are we all just hurtling toward a meaningless death?

Through the din of these frantic questions, you hear a gentle whisper—maybe not the thunderclap you wanted. It's a still, small voice that teases your heart. "You are my child."

That changes everything. There's your identity. There you find both past and future.

66. Behind Us All the Way

> So do not fear, for I am with you;
> do not be dismayed, for I am your God.

> I will strengthen you and help you;
> I will uphold you with my righteous right hand.
> —ISAIAH 41:10

Have you ever taught a child to ride a bike? It can be quite scary for both parties. At first the adult generally pushes the bike, walking alongside it. Gradually the child takes control. At a certain point the child is pedaling and steering, but the adult still has a hand on the bike, ready to hold it up if it starts to fall. Even after letting go, the adult stays close behind, ready to rush in if needed.

That could be a picture of God's support for us. At times we might think we're riding all alone, but he promises to be right behind us, ready to help.

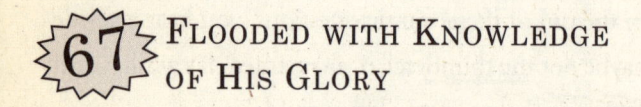

67 Flooded with Knowledge of His Glory

> For the earth will be filled with the
> knowledge of the glory of the LORD,
> as the waters cover the sea.
> —HABAKKUK 2:14

The prophet Habakkuk had some complaints to deliver. God had some explaining to do. For one thing, Habakkuk's cries for help had gone unanswered for too long. Injustice ran rampant. Then when God did decide to act, he used the wicked, ruthless nation of Babylon to punish his people. That made no sense at all. Habakkuk issued his challenge and waited "to see what he will say to me" (verse 1).

The Lord's answer was larger than the question. Babylon itself would be punished in due time, because even their military might could never keep God from filling the earth with his glory. No matter how bleak the current moment appears, God's glory will eventually be known everywhere.

68 SHINING BRIGHT

> Commit your way to the LORD;
>   trust in him and he will do this:
> He will make your righteousness shine like the dawn,
>   the justice of your cause like the noonday sun.
> Be still before the LORD and wait patiently for him;
>   do not fret when men succeed in their ways,
>   when they carry out their wicked schemes.
>
> —PSALM 37:5–7

We sometimes complain about bad things happening to good people, but the flip side is also problematic—when good things happen to bad people. We see cheaters prospering. We see the violent grabbing power. We see high-level swindlers sparking an economic crisis that threatens all of us good, hard-working folks. That just isn't right.

"Be still," the psalmist says. "Wait patiently." In time your good life will brighten the world. Meanwhile, keep committing yourself to live God's way.

6 Challenges in Your Work and Service

You get passed over for a promotion. Your company merges and you drop a few rungs on the corporate ladder. The project you spearheaded gets sabotaged. Your boss is a real jerk, and you get blamed for his mistakes. Or you've started your own business, and it's taking far more time to be profitable than you expected. Little mistakes are becoming major issues. You're finding it hard to compete morally in a cutthroat world.

Maybe your work is at home, caring for children and creating an environment of growth and love, but you feel overworked and underappreciated. Or maybe your biggest challenges involve church work. Your volunteers are jumping ship. Your youth-group social was a fiasco. You find that you're really not cut out for teaching second-grade Sunday school. You might think that God would guarantee success of all efforts done for him, but that doesn't seem to be the case.

Many of God's promises involve the work we do each day and how we do it. We encounter some of our greatest difficulties in that sphere of life, and we desperately need some divine support.

69. Thorny Situation

> But he said to me, "My grace is sufficient for you,
> for my power is made perfect in weakness."
> Therefore I will boast all the more gladly about my
> weaknesses, so that Christ's power may rest on me.
> —2 Corinthians 12:9

Paul had a problem, but we're not sure what it was. He called it his thorn in the flesh. Was it encroaching blindness, epileptic attacks, migraine headaches? Whatever it was, he prayed three times for its removal, but God said no. And here we read his reasoning.

Astonishingly, God doesn't need servants who are perfectly strong. He wants weak servants who rely on his strength. If you're beating yourself up over some personal failure and blaming it on some flaw in your character, take note. You can boast in your weakness and grab hold of Christ's power.

70. Building Plans

> "For I know the plans I have for you," declares the
> Lord, "plans to prosper you and not to harm you, plans
> to give you hope and a future. Then you will call upon
> me and come and pray to me, and I will listen to you."
> —Jeremiah 29:11–12

A young executive thrills to hear the boss say, "We have big plans for you." A student walks taller when a teacher says, "You have a great future ahead of you." Imagine how it feels when the Creator of the universe says that.

The Israelites had been punished for their idolatry, exiled for seventy years in Babylon. This is God's make-up message. He had not forgotten them. He was planning big things for their future. They would soon return to their land and rebuild it.

We can grab this message for ourselves. God plans to build us up too.

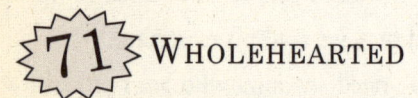

71. WHOLEHEARTED

> Whatever you do, work at it with all your heart,
> as working for the Lord, not for men,
> since you know that you will receive
> an inheritance from the Lord as a reward.
> It is the Lord Christ you are serving.
> —COLOSSIANS 3:23–24

On a scorchingly hot day, one bricklayer said to another, "Slow down, buddy. The boss is gone for the day."

The other man, a Christian, replied, "I'm not working for *him*."

This is a promise that can transform our daily work. Whether we're laying bricks or pushing paper, keeping house or hawking wares, we ultimately do our work for the Lord, and he deserves our best effort. This also implies that we need to put Christ's values into practice—loving the people we work with, humbly serving others, making sure our work honors the Lord. And we're promised something more than a paycheck—an eternal reward.

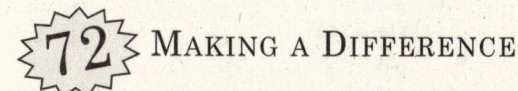

72 Making a Difference

> But as for you, be strong and do not give up,
> for your work will be rewarded.
> —2 Chronicles 15:7

King Asa was trying to make a difference. The nation had descended into sin and idolatry, neglecting the worship of the Lord. Even members of the royal family were building idols, but Asa put a stop to that. He tried to turn the people's hearts back to God, but it was a daunting task.

At one point, a prophet was sent to Asa with this promise. His reforming work would be rewarded. As challenging as it was, the king's effort had come to God's attention, and he appreciated it.

If you have taken on a challenging ministry, don't despair. Even if it's progressing slowly, know that God sees what you're doing and will reward you. You can make a difference.

73. Eagles' Wings

> But those who hope in the LORD
>> will renew their strength.
>> They will soar on wings like eagles;
>> they will run and not grow weary,
>> they will walk and not be faint.
>> —ISAIAH 40:31

Doing good work takes a lot out of you. Whether you're trying to run a business or serving in ministry, if you're pouring your soul into the effort, you'll get weary. That feeling intensifies if you think no one cares what you're doing.

The Jews during the Babylonian captivity felt like that, complaining, "My cause is disregarded by my God" (verse 27). But the Lord sent them this promise to lift them out of their doldrums. He would strengthen the weary. If they would dare to put their hope in him, he would help them not just to walk or run but to soar!

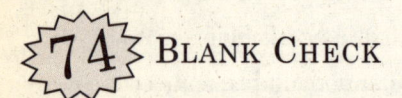

74. Blank Check

> I can do everything through him
>> who gives me strength.
>> —PHILIPPIANS 4:13

Don't test this promise by jumping off a roof. You can't fly, no matter how much strength God gives you. This is not some spiritual blank check that will make you a superhero. The apostle Paul was talking about the circumstances of his life and ministry. Because he trusted the Lord, he could be content in good situations and bad. God gave him strength to deal with everything.

That's still a powerful promise for you, because you have a lot to deal with. You face disgruntled workers, financial crises, mechanical glitches, and power struggles. Commit yourself to the Lord, working his way, and he will give you the strength to handle these challenges.

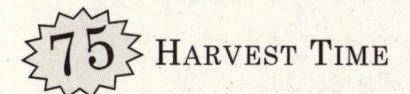

75. Harvest Time

> Let us not become weary in doing good,
> for at the proper time we will reap
> a harvest if we do not give up.
> —Galatians 6:9

If you have ever taught a child about how plants grow, you probably got a fresh insight into how amazing that process is. A seed goes into the soil, drops roots, and then sprouts upward. Soon there's a plant that's several times larger than the original seed.

The child is likely to look for the sprout the day after planting.

And the next day. And the next. Sometimes it's hard to grasp the length of time necessary for growth to occur.

That's hard for some adults to grasp as well. If you've been working hard and haven't seen results yet, this promise is for you. *At the proper time* the harvest will be ready, so be patient.

76 Beyond Our Wildest Dreams

> Now to him who is able to do immeasurably more
> than all we ask or imagine, according to his
> power that is at work within us, to him be glory
> in the church and in Christ Jesus throughout
> all generations, for ever and ever! Amen.
> —Ephesians 3:20–21

Ancient Israel had the ark of the covenant, representing God's presence, but some folks began to think that God was contained in it.

The Pharisees had their religious laws, twisted to their purposes.

The pagans babbled repetitive prayers to force their gods into action. Jesus gave us the Lord's Prayer as an alternative, but we often just babble that, as if its repetition will force our God into action.

In every generation, people try to reduce God to a formula, an icon, a system, a statement, but he consistently breaks out of any box we make for him. Thank God!

77. The Manual

> I will instruct you and teach you in the way you
> should go;
> I will counsel you and watch over you.
> —Psalm 32:8

One of the frustrating things about computers these days is that you don't get a manual. Well, it's *in* the computer somewhere, or online, but you don't really need it until your computer breaks down, and then you can't get to it.

The Lord promises that he won't leave us so directionless. This promise speaks not only of teaching but also mentoring, involving observation and advice.

If you're involved in ministry, you know the challenges that come constantly. It's always an improvisation, and you never feel fully prepared. That's why it's so important to have both God's instruction and his ongoing counsel. He's there to help each step of the way.

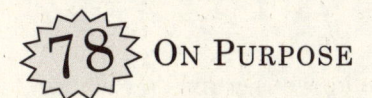

78. On Purpose

> And we know that in all things God works
> for the good of those who love him, who have
> been called according to his purpose.
> —Romans 8:28

This promise is familiar to many. It's the go-to verse for comfort in hard times. Some might consider it overused. When you're reeling from some tragedy, the last thing you want to hear is that it's really good for you—even if that is true.

But we often miss the very end of that promise, and this is what makes it especially helpful. God has a purpose for us, and that purpose will not be thwarted. Calamities cause us pain, but they cannot derail God's plans. He takes bad events and braids them into his good direction for our lives.

As you serve his purpose in your life, take heart in this assurance.

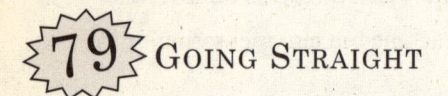

79. Going Straight

> Trust in the LORD with all your heart
> and lean not on your own understanding;
> in all your ways acknowledge him,
> and he will make your paths straight.
> —Proverbs 3:5–6

In business, the smartest thing is to know what you don't know. Companies hire consultants to steer their decisions in certain matters. Executives could pretend to know, making guesses based on partial knowledge, and some do. But the smart ones listen to the experts and yield to those who know better.

Who knows better than the Lord? When it comes to living life, what better expert could there be than the Author of life? Why would we lean on our own understanding when we can get clear direction from our Creator?

When we consult him on daily decisions, we avoid the mistakes that would cause zigzags and backtracks. We move straight ahead on his path.

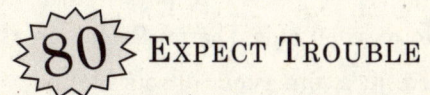

80. Expect Trouble

> I have told you these things, so that in me you
> may have peace. In this world you will have trouble.
> But take heart! I have overcome the world.
> —John 16:33

Maybe you consider yourself an expert in Murphy's Law—if anything can go wrong, it will. Maybe your home life or job has been marked by troubles. Sure, you've probably made some mistakes along the way, but there's usually a pack of bad luck involved, not to mention opposition from others.

This would come as no surprise to Jesus, who told his disciples to expect trouble. But that's never the end of the story. We can find peace even in our setbacks because we know Jesus wins. When we know we are serving Christ, we know that his plan goes forward, regardless of any bumps in the road.

81. Open Hand, Open Heart

> Give generously to him [your needy brother] and
> do so without a grudging heart; then because of
> this the LORD your God will bless you in all your
> work and in everything you put your hand to.
> —DEUTERONOMY 15:10

When money is tight, it's hard to let go of it. That makes it even more important to make generosity a cornerstone of your life and work. According to this promise, when you open your hand and heart to the needy, you are practicing a business principle that leads to success.

You can't give what you don't have, but what do you have? Can you invite people over for meals? Can you volunteer your time? Can you share your social capital, networking with others to provide legal, medical, dental, financial, repair, or educational services to the needy?

If you're committed to generosity, you'll find a way.

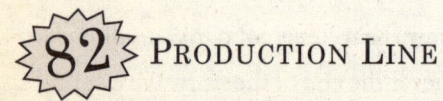

82. Production Line

> Make every effort to add to your faith goodness; and to
> goodness, knowledge; and to knowledge, self-control; and to
> self-control, perseverance; and to perseverance, godliness; and

> to godliness, brotherly kindness; and to brotherly kindness, love. For if you possess these qualities in increasing measure, they will keep you from being ineffective and unproductive in your knowledge of our Lord Jesus Christ.
> —2 Peter 1:5–8

Peter uses some surprisingly business-oriented terms. How often do you talk about being effective and productive in your knowledge of Jesus? Yet that's what we're called to.

Scripture always puts knowing and doing together. Don't just know the truth, do it. A quick trip through this lineup of qualities shows that they're all active. The Spirit grows these qualities in our lives, and as a result we make a difference in our world.

83 The Firm

> If the LORD delights in a man's way,
> he makes his steps firm;
> though he stumble, he will not fall,
> for the LORD upholds him with his hand.
> —Psalm 37:23–24

David lived in the mountains, foothills, and canyons of Palestine. The terrain was tough. Along the craggy passes and dirt roads, it was hard to find firm footing—and very easy to stumble. So it's understandable that the psalmist would use that metaphor in a spiritual way. If the Lord likes where you're going, he helps you get there.

That's worth considering in your daily work. Does the Lord delight in what you do each day? You don't have to be a missionary or pastor. If you just make widgets, do you honor God in *how* you make them, in your diligence, your attitude, and your teamwork?

7 When You Lose a Loved One

One of the toughest of tough times is the departure of a close relative or dear friend. We miss them, their look, their touch, their talk. We can't fathom that they won't be there for us any longer.

Sometimes we worry about the pain they might have felt in their final days or moments. Sometimes we grieve about their unfinished business. No matter how many years people have, they always seem to die too young. Sometimes the experience makes us worry about our own inevitable death, and this can spark a host of spiritual questions.

The Bible treats death as a sad component of the human condition, the legacy of Adam and Eve. It is a force to be reckoned with. And yet Jesus *has* reckoned with it and emerged victorious. For the believer, death has lost its teeth. It cannot devour our future hopes.

But it is still sad to say good-bye. We live in this in-between time, anticipating eternal life but still under death's sway. And so we grieve, but not as those who have no hope. We bemoan our separation from those we love, and we devote ourselves to tears for a time, but then we remember our ultimate victory.

84. Bless You

> Blessed are those who mourn,
> for they will be comforted.
> —Matthew 5:4

When people heard Jesus preach the Sermon on the Mount, they were astonished. He started with nine blessings that were the opposite of what people expected. How could you declare mourners happy? Or those who are poor or hungry or persecuted? But together, they form a pattern. Those who endure hardship in this life have a special relationship with God, which will yield great benefits.

As for mourning, there's no denying the sorrow of the moment. When you have lost a precious friend or relative, you are deeply wounded. But you also receive comfort from the people around you. New relationships are formed and strengthened. Most important is that God himself offers comfort. Your time of grief may become an opportunity for renewed closeness with the Lord.

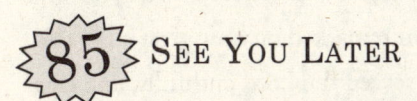

85. See You Later

> Now is your time of grief, but I will see
> you again and you will rejoice, and no
> one will take away your joy.
> —John 16:22

Jesus was preparing his disciples. Hours after he said this, he would be arrested. Within a day he would be crucified. And surely he was hinting at his resurrection, which would bring great joy. But it wouldn't be long before he would leave them again, for heaven.

He could be saying this to you: "Now is your time of grief." It is good and right to mourn for a loved one. Don't let anyone tell you that tears are out of order. We have a right to miss those who pass on.

Yet this is not the end. We anticipate a future reunion filled with joy. Because of Jesus's resurrection, we look forward to a resurrected life with him.

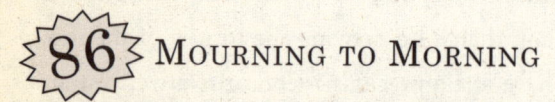

86. Mourning to Morning

> Weeping may remain for a night,
> but rejoicing comes in the morning.
> —Psalm 30:5

The family was going to the funeral of their one-hundred-year-old grandmother. Each one of them remarked on how great a life this woman had enjoyed. She had served the Lord faithfully, and this funeral would be a joyous time to celebrate her life and witness.

Then the youngest daughter spoke up. "Yeah, but I'm sad. I miss her." That seemed to free up the others to voice their sorrows as well.

Weeping is perfectly appropriate "for a night," and that night might last weeks or even months. We shouldn't feel constrained to put a happy face on a sad situation. But at a certain point the tears are spent and the morning dawns. Then we rejoice in the life of the person we had the privilege to know.

87 Death Valley

> Even though I walk
>   through the valley of the shadow of death,
> I will fear no evil,
> for you are with me;
> your rod and your staff,
> they comfort me.
>
> —Psalm 23:4

The Twenty-third Psalm gives us vivid images that start with sheep-herding and goes far beyond. What is the "valley of the shadow of death"? Was it some dark canyon David knew in the Judean desert near Bethlehem? Or was he envisioning some otherworldly experience? Or both?

We don't know much about death, but we can easily imagine it as a shadowy valley. And what a comfort to know that we don't have to walk through it alone. We can encounter death without fear, because the Lord, our eternal Shepherd, goes with us even on that final journey.

88. Do You Believe This?

> I am the resurrection and the life. He who
> believes in me will live, even though he dies;
> and whoever lives and believes in me will
> never die. Do you believe this?
> —John 11:25–26

Martha was mourning the death of her brother, Lazarus. She had hoped for his healing, but Jesus arrived too late. When she expressed her disappointment, this was Jesus's answer.

He's clearly talking about eternal life. The believer will live "even though he dies." The trust connection with Jesus opens up a resurrected life beyond death. After saying this, Jesus brought Lazarus back to life, a powerful sign that he had power over death, physically and spiritually.

"Do you believe this?" Jesus asked Martha, who responded with a stirring confession of faith. Do *you* believe this? If we truly see Jesus holding the power of resurrection, it transforms our view of death—and life.

89. What We Will Be

> Dear friends, now we are children of God,
> and what we will be has not yet been made known.

> But we know that when he appears, we shall
> be like him, for we shall see him as he is.
> —1 JOHN 3:2

For a believer, physical death is the passage to a different kind of life. While God has given some insight into what his future kingdom will be like, there's still a lot we don't know. John confesses that we don't know "what we will be." Other Scriptures hint that we will have an imperishable body, perhaps something like what Jesus had after his resurrection. John confirms that "we shall be like him."

Overall, we can look forward to a greater level of intimacy with God, seeing him "as he is." So we can truly rejoice when others take that step.

90. Sabbath Rest

> There remains, then, a Sabbath-rest for the people
> of God; for anyone who enters God's rest also rests
> from his own work, just as God did from his. Let us,
> therefore, make every effort to enter that rest.
> —HEBREWS 4:9–11

God created the world in six days and rested on the seventh. That's why he established the seventh day as a Sabbath, a day when his people could rest from their labors. But the author of Hebrews sees that "rest" in another way. It is God's kingdom. It is salvation. It is our future life with God.

Of course we talk about the final rest of those who pass on, but it's not just some soul sleep. According to Hebrews, when a believer dies, we might say that she reached her Sabbath day, a time of relaxation and restoration enjoyed with our Creator.

91. In His Grip

> I give them eternal life, and they shall never perish;
> no one can snatch them out of my hand. My Father,
> who has given them to me, is greater than all;
> no one can snatch them out of my Father's hand.
> —John 10:28–29

Well into her nineties, Ellen was still thinking clearly—until she went on a particular pain medication. Suddenly her thoughts were scattered, and she was mean and critical. Her family was appalled. This was not the sweet, godly Ellen they knew.

Sometimes, as people near death, they might do or say things that spark spiritual worries. What if they have a nasty argument and never confess it? What if they express deep doubts about God?

Jesus assures us that he keeps a tight grip on his followers. We need not worry about the eternal destiny of those who have committed their lives to him.

92. We're Not Making This Up

> "No eye has seen,
>   no ear has heard,
> no mind has conceived
>   what God has prepared for those who love
> him"—but God has revealed it to us by his Spirit.
> —1 CORINTHIANS 2:9–10

This promise is often misunderstood. The poetry, borrowed from Isaiah, is usually taken to mean that we can never know the fullness of what God has prepared for us, that it is beyond our senses, inconceivable. But the apostle Paul adds that God *has* revealed this to us. Because of the Spirit's communication with us, we *do* know what's in store.

Paul's main point is the radical difference between the world's wisdom and God's. The story of salvation, the love of God, and our eternal reward—these are not things the world would make up. They are mysteries that only God's Spirit could share.

93. Win-Win

> For to me, to live is Christ and to die is gain.
> —PHILIPPIANS 1:21

Paul felt he was nearing death, and he welcomed it, well aware of the promise that to die was to "be with Christ, which is better by far" (verse 23). Elsewhere he wrote about being "absent from the body" and thus "present with the Lord" (2 Corinthians 5:8, KJV). He wasn't worried about his destination.

But he was still torn. If he lived on, he could do much more work for the Lord. Essentially he was faced with two good options: being with Christ or living for Christ. It was a win-win.

We can understand both sides as we mourn for believers who have passed. Their death is truly gain, as they bask in Christ's presence, while we have the opportunity to keep living our lives for Christ.

94. Devising Ways

> Like water spilled on the ground, which cannot be recovered, so we must die. But God does not take away life; instead, he devises ways so that a banished person may not remain estranged from him.
> —2 Samuel 14:14

A wise woman said this to David regarding his rebellious son, Absalom, but this teaches us something important. We can ultimately rejoice in the deaths of Christians, but what can we say about someone who has never expressed faith in Christ? That is an especially painful situation.

David's wise woman gives us a hint of hope. God doesn't want people to perish eternally. He "devises ways" to restore his relationship with people.

We don't know what happens in the last breath, in the final thoughts of a dying person. We can hope that God has devised a way to invite a person to himself in that moment.

95. Present Tents

> Now we know that if the earthly tent we live
> in is destroyed, we have a building from God,
> an eternal house in heaven, not built by human
> hands. Meanwhile we groan, longing to be
> clothed with our heavenly dwelling.
> —2 Corinthians 5:1–2

The apostle Paul knew tents. When he wasn't preaching, he made tents. He had to pay the bills somehow, and we can imagine that tents were rather popular. Travel was easy in the first-century Roman Empire, with good roads and safe seas. A well-made, portable, temporary lodging would be good to have.

So it's fitting for Paul to talk about the human body as a tent.

No matter how well made it is, the body is still temporary. We are traveling an earthly road, but we're headed for a heavenly home. There we will move into an eternal house, with a divine builder.

96 REDEEMED

> But God will redeem my life from the grave;
> he will surely take me to himself.
> —PSALM 49:15

Many of the psalms depict a face-off between the haves and the have-nots. The psalmist is always on the poorer side of that divide, often bemoaning how the rich keep getting richer, often at the expense of the poor. (Some things never change.)

Death is the great equalizer. No matter how much wealth you have collected, you have to leave it behind. "No man can redeem the life of another," this psalmist says. "No payment is ever enough" (verses 7–8).

After death, the roles are reversed, and there is usually some last-laugh glee in the psalmist's tone. Wicked rich folks die and decay, but the righteous poor live in God's presence, enjoying his eternal wealth.

Maybe no human has enough money to buy back a life, but God does.

97. LOVE GIFT

> For God so loved the world that he gave his one
> and only Son, that whoever believes in him shall not
> perish but have eternal life. For God did not send
> his Son into the world to condemn the world,
> but to save the world through him.
>
> —JOHN 3:16–17

Our Creator loves the world he created, longing to be in relationship with each person. But we know that love is more than a feeling—love acts—and so God showed his love in a dramatic way. He gave his Son, the one and only.

As a result, we have the promise of life forever, if only we believe. We don't merely believe *that* this is true; we believe *in* this person. Believing *in* involves trust, commitment, participation.

Then there is life beyond death, joy transforming sorrow, and hope in the face of despair.

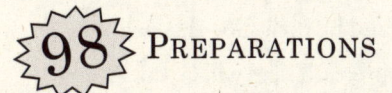

98. PREPARATIONS

> In my Father's house are many rooms; if it were
> not so, I would have told you. I am going there to
> prepare a place for you. And if I go and prepare a

> place for you, I will come back and take you
> to be with me that you also may be where I am.
> —John 14:2–3

Keith moved across the country for a new job, and this meant uprooting his family. He made the move first, house hunting in his off-hours, preparing a place for his wife and kids. For them it was weird. They were home, but waiting for a future home. They prepared to say good-bye to their friends, though they weren't sure when they'd have to. And they missed Keith.

Do you get the picture? Jesus has gone to prepare our future home. The loved one you're mourning has now made that move, with sad good-byes, but also joy.

99. No More Tears

> And I heard a loud voice from the throne saying,
> "Now the dwelling of God is with men, and he will
> live with them. They will be his people, and God
> himself will be with them and be their God. He will
> wipe every tear from their eyes. There will be no
> more death or mourning or crying or pain, for the
> old order of things has passed away."
> —Revelation 21:3–4

We look forward with longing to that future time when God makes all things new. Our bodies groan, along with all creation, for that final transformation. There is much we don't know about how this will happen, but Scripture gives us glimpses of heavenly bliss. The full reality of it would probably blow our minds.

Central to this vision is our togetherness with God. He will be moving in with us, and we with him.

More 99 Ways for only $5.99!

99 Ways to Increase Your Income
Frank Martin

99 Ways to Stretch Your Home Budget
Cheri Gillard

99 Ways to Fight Worry and Stress
Elsa Kok Colopy

99 Ways to Entertain Your Family for Free
Mack Thomas

99 Ways to Build Job Security
Gary Nowinski

99 Bible Promises for Tough Times
Randy Petersen

In challenging times we all need advice on how to overcome stress and find encouragement. The 99 Ways books offer up-to-date, practical, and reliable information in a succinct format at a price anyone can afford.

WATERBROOK PRESS
www.waterbrookmultnomah.com